THROWING CATS AT THE SKY

THROWING CATS AT THE SKY

TROY O'BRIEN

Burlington, Vermont

Copyright © 2020 by Troy O'Brien

All rights reserved. No part of this publication may be reproduced, distributed, or transmitted in any form or by any means, including photocopying, recording, or other electronic or mechanical methods, without the prior written permission of the publisher, except in the case of brief quotations embodied in critical reviews and certain other noncommercial uses permitted by copyright law.

Onion River Press
191 Bank Street
Burlington, VT 05401

ISBN: 978-1-949066-18-0

Printed in the United States of America

To Edda, the brightest thing in my life.

CONTENTS

dedication	v
Rabid Poe	1
Unmoored	3
Crooked Smiles	5
Uncommon	7
Solemn	9
Playgrounds	11
Soft	13
Untitled	15
Throwing Cats at the Sky	17
Hollow	19
Thorns	21
Standards	23
Measurements	25

Stones	27
Fences	29
Watched	31
Crescendo at Huntington Gorge	33
Fields	35
Chances	37
Deeper Waters	39
Trolls	41

Rabid Poe

A child I imagined rabies
A disease of bees
circling the head
firing beams of light

A student
already old beyond my years
I read that Poe likely died rabid

Now after the all too rapid
decline of years
I wonder what Poe thought
of bees

Unmoored

It drifted and dead sailors manned it
A small yacht
old

They climbed the rigging
Tying with fingers that remembered
they sailed again

They looked for old horizons
Things they could
never walk again

The wind flows over them
the waves lap
and they wish for mooring

Crooked Smiles

I never saw a dog with a crooked smile
More's the pity

if I had
it would have lit up my life
like fireworks

A feral look and a crooked smile
in a bar

odd
something so commonplace can feel so singular

As if wolves were uncommon
and the night a rarity

Send that smile over to me
see what you might get

Uncommon

Is it specific
to look for the odd
and I wonder how the common
becomes a lifestyle

I haven't seen a praying mantis in years
lime green and predatory
to see them as a boy

Watching glass melt in a fire pit
Lightning storms from mountains
these are not singular
but sought and wyrd plays its part

and I wonder how much commonality
we can have
how much the weird
isn't

and why a car accident makes people talk
more than a luna moth

how uncommon does it have to be
how rare to trigger old wiring
I'd ask you to tell me
but that would make it common

Solemn

I've never really been solemn
Never had a taste for it

Feels like an actor
wearing a hat
Blake said exuberance is beauty
I find beauty in this

We brought a body
To Mystic Canada
For burial

There were two men there
one to bury him
trees with black bare branches
dropped melting snow in the sun

A sole mourner wore a suit
He may have had a medal
on his coat
I forget

He did have a cane
We gave the digger two American dollars as a tip
after we lowered the burial vault in the grave
He looked grateful
Customs didn't give us a hard time either way

Playgrounds

There was
something I lost

I don't know what it was
unimportant

I turned and it was the sky
I'd left it behind

You give up the swing
A child grown now

The world doesn't tilt anymore
The ferris wheel is shut
The ticket taker
long gone

Soft

The edge of shadow
is rarely blurred
but it moves in wind under trees

proceed softly now
like the first brush of a hand
on a woman's thigh

like you were approaching a
mirror when you know something
wrong

the step that creaks when you
came home a drunk teenager
how did you turn your heel
so no one would hear
do you remember?

or is it as soft as memory?
the line between light and shadow
gone

Untitled

The world shown down on the sun

blue and green staring on fire
and it was well

wish the fire would slip away
wish for a cold dark heart
you'll get them

stir the embers
wish it hadn't ended this way
not with a bang
but a two minute poem

Throwing Cats at the Sky

As a hobby
It seems there are so many ways to do it

One handed by the tail
might be fun
especially if you just snatched it off the ground
no warnings
the resulting noises would be entirely worth the
        effort

Or you could do it mechanically
arrange a small catapult
or trebuchet

Set them on a small pillow
and thwang
there goes Fluffy

Consider the skies you could do it under
mark less blue
starry night
thunder and rain so hard you can't see
dusk
dawn

I'd just keep trying it
to see if one time
an out stretched

claw

would snag on a star
a lightning bolt
or a cloud

and the cat would howl
wondering how to get
down

Hollow

Sometimes a hollow October madness
takes me and I
scratch tree hand fingers across a sky
bright with stars

cut your hand
on a corn leaf dry and pale yellow
and rustling

don't search for narratives here
harvest moon
whiskey and snow
it paints the mountains first
white and grey with exposed rock
and barren seems a comfort

touch the leafless tree
in the wind
touch the sky

Thorns

My best memories
are hooked and black
dripping rain in the spring
on blackberry vines

I loved being torn by them
And the marks they left
picking the berries

my hands are covered
in scars

those are the only ones
I'm fond of

Standards

Set your cloth up on poles
Red with tools
Green with religion
Multicolored with stars

Carry them in the heat at Gettysburg
To focus the nearly dead on their leaders
With bugle horns to carry them on their way

Put a horse's mane outside a tent
on a stick
conquer the world

Call them banners

Paint them on walls with hardware spray paint
This street is ours
Paint the dead
Yours and theirs
Triumphs and losses

Set your standard high
Consider weapons
and go

Why not?
Everyone else does it

Measurements

Mark the world in increments
if you like

how is your world measured?
Coffee cups, teaspoons or bottles of beer

Bright fall mornings brown leaves all around
and a shotgun
and wings

or the tedious monitoring
of accumulated specie

Or is it the year you didn't
go back to Big Sur to see
Henry's Library again
in redwoods

They are all of them
yesterday spaces

Measured?

I'd rather be flipping rocks for crayfish
in a cold stream

Who the fuck are you anyway?
To be so pretentious
to miss the breaking leaf

Stones

What lives under the stones
I've seen grouse hop off
An intersection

Walls so old the hill farm
is gone

Barb wire grown into trees

Slept in the snow deer hunting

Swing that shotgun swift
young man
And make it count

Fences

birds ignore them

Watched

I am being watched
Can they see the mark
of deviance
or do they see
the suit

Too many times I think
Do the delicious sounds
Still vibrate in the aether
I cannot hear them
a new iteration must be born

The doorman lets me in
He glances at my white toothed smile
He didn't notice the suit

I walk the hall to my room
My neighbor opens her door
Same as mine

She looks into my eyes
She asks if I would like
A glass of wine

Her eye are violet
I smile and say yes

She doesn't look at
the suit
No one but she
Watches in her apartment

Is the mark in my eyes
Does she watch
She pours the wine
I taste
and smile

Crescendo at Huntington Gorge

The maple leaves on the ground are soft with rain
It is early summer
The rain is softer under the trees on the walk in

It drips off green leaves slowly
The ground has grey roots above
Where they fight to split ledge

We exit the woods into the rain
The ledges over the gorge are wet and dark grey
We sit, the two of us with a twelve pack in the rain

Beers pop with rain sliding down the sides of the cans
The river is very high

White crests most of it as it falls
Down a series of stepped pools

The vibration is so strong
We feel it through the stone we sit on
Darker clouds are coming
Black wings race ahead of them

Thunder sounds in the distance
That so much sensation
Could come from the dance of particles
Seems impossible

I call it the devil's argument
We sit on thrumming rock made mostly of
    empty space
And think of the dead who drowned here
My friend says he can see lightning dancing
On the tips of his fingers

I remark that if he concentrates enough
Maybe he can shoot it
The rain comes harder
The lightning closer

The blue fork comes down
Flash and sound simultaneous
Symphony

Fields

My neighbor grew popcorn
Below fall harvest moons
We pulled up the rustling stalks
Stacked them in a cart

If I could recall the smell of the time
crisp
autumnal

The sights
silver yellow light long shadows
Rustling wind
made up harvest songs

The van rolls past feed corn stalks
It is October and the moon is full and yellow

Would it be enough to pull over
To cut my hand under the moon
On a pale corn leaf and see the blood
Rustling and dripping finely

As if everything was one again
I kept on driving

Chances

How many have you taken?
How many times have you been burned?

Poker is a game of chance
And strategy

I went to Devil's Gore once
I waited for an hour to see if he
would cut a deal
He didn't show up

It was full of ankle busting crags
I liked that

Take your chances
Savor them

Deeper Waters

Sun Tzu said there was
A time for quiet contemplation
and a time for rapid action
I gave up that chance for rapid action
when it really mattered

Now I wish I had chose
differently

I wish I was twelve again
fishing in a pond

There was an old willow there
Lying down in the pond
still alive
We used to climb it
And spot the bass
Tell the other kids where to cast

Cast well
And hook a big one

Trolls

When I was a child
We used to sled down a hill
Surrounded by blackberries

I used to pick them so my mother
could make blackberry pie

I wore a denim coat to wade into them
I don't even know
if they make them any more

I pushed my brother of the trail one day
sledding behind him
He pushed his teeth
through his lower lip
broke a couple of them

There was a
rotten pine
at the top of the hill

In fading light
It looked like a troll

www.ingramcontent.com/pod-product-compliance
Lightning Source LLC
Chambersburg PA
CBHW030140100526
44592CB00011B/979